Mrs. Patricia Pogue
1101 Richard Rd.
CA

D0392379

THE CAPITALIST
CODE

THE CAPITALIST CODE

*It Can Save Your Life
(and Make You Very Rich!)*

BEN STEIN

Humanix Books
The Capitalist Code

Copyright © 2017 by Ben Stein
All rights reserved

Humanix Books, P.O. Box 20989, West Palm Beach, FL 33416, USA
www.humanixbooks.com | info@humanixbooks.com

Library of Congress Control Number: 2017941400

No part of this book may be reproduced or transmitted in any form or by any means, electronic or mechanical, including photocopying, recording, or by any other information storage and retrieval system, without written permission from the publisher.

Cover Photo: Getty Images Inc. Stock # 183078716
Cover Design: Paul McCarthy
Interior Design: Scribe Inc.

Humanix Books is a division of Humanix Publishing, LLC. Its trademark, consisting of the words "Humanix" is registered in the Patent and Trademark Office and in other countries.

Disclaimer: The information presented in this book is meant to be used for general resource purposes only; it is not intended as specific financial advice for any individual and should not substitute financial advice from a finance professional.

ISBN: 978-1-63006-084-8 (Hardcover)
ISBN: 978-1-63006-085-5 (E-book)

Printed in the United States of America
10 9 8 7 6 5 4 3 2

CONTENTS

DEDICATION

For my Wife for Life, Alex

ACKNOWLEDGMENTS

For the ultimate guide, friend and mentor, Warren E. Buffett, for my frequent colleague and advisor, Phil DeMuth, and for my pals at Merrill Lynch, Kevin Hanley and Jerry Au.

CHAPTER ONE

IT'S NEVER TOO EARLY FOR THE TRUTH

Tis strange but true; for the truth is always strange;
Stranger than fiction.

—Lord Byron

It's time for some important truths in your lives. It's never too early for the truth. But first, who am I to presume to tell you the truth?

Young Americans, you know me. In some ways, I am the most well-known teacher of economics in the world. It's not because I know the most about economics. In point of fact, hardly anyone knows anything about economics. There are a jillion people on TV who will tell you they know about economics. Mr. Trump told us he knew about economics; Mrs. Clinton told us she knew about economics. But they didn't—and almost no one can—predict the future of the United States economy with even a tiny bit of exactitude, if that is what is commonly understood to be the main ability of economists.

No one ever could; the economy is fantastically complex. Trying to understand it is like trying to predict the weather or read the minds of the eight billion souls on this earth.

WHAT ECONOMISTS KNOW

I am a superfamous teacher of economics not because of any books or formulas I have written, although I have written many books about economics and finance, including some complex ones mostly authored by my genius friend Phil DeMuth. No, I am famous because Hollywood grabbed me up by the scruff of my neck, threw me around, shone lights on me, and rolled film on me. I played the boring economics teacher in one of the most magnificent movie comedies ever made, *Ferris Bueller's Day Off*. I'm the one who asks, "Bueller, Bueller?" when taking attendance and who tells bored students about the "Smoot-Hawley Tariff Act" while they fall asleep at their desks and drool onto the Formica desktops.

In fact, I'm not an actor by education either, although I have been in hundreds of TV shows and movies. I am trained as an economist (and a lawyer). As I told you, this does not mean that I know with any precision the direction of the U.S. economy, why unemployment is high or low, or especially the direction of stock or commodity prices—neither does anyone else. No Democrat or Republican, man or woman, old or young, can tell the future. It's a rare one who can even speak with the slightest truthfulness about the present. Economists are like psychiatrists; they have theories and ideas and data. But they can prove little.

Economics is about the allocation of scarce goods, chiefly the scarce good known as "money." I want to assure you that economists know, in general, which moves make money and which don't. They know, for example, that working is usually (but not always) a better path to prosperity than idleness. They know that trade protectionism sounds good but provides few benefits or none at all.

But that knowledge rarely makes them rich. A rich economist, at least one who has gotten rich from economics, is a rare bird indeed.

Neither myself nor economists as a group are experts in finding hidden gems among stocks. Alas, none of us can pick out the stocks that will be the next Apple or Facebook—no one can. At least, no one can for certain. The woods are filled with men and women who will take your money pretending they can pick stocks consistently. With only a few exceptions, they're not leveling with you.

THE TRUTH ABOUT CAPITALISM
IN THE UNITED STATES

But I can tell you some things of value. You are being sold a false bill of goods about money, about the world you live in, and about how to give yourself a bright future, money-wise. Let's start with the obvious: When your professors and your schoolmates tell you that capitalism as we see it in the United States of America right now is an evil, exploitive system, they're lying. When they tell you that you're being consistently ripped off by Wall Street, they're lying and they're hurting you.

In fact, the system of democratic capitalism as now practiced in the U.S.A. is the best, brightest, most hopeful plan for organizing human economic activity that there has ever been. This is true both for you as an individual and for your whole generation. Capitalism is a great supermachine that can put in smart people and groups as ordinary students and workers and take them out as well-to-do happy campers.

Capitalism, if you play the game by the most sensible rules, is like having a neighborhood or dorm basketball game on the local courts—where the stakes are lunch money—and being allowed to have LeBron James on your team.

Free market, regulated capitalism is like handing everyone entering the labor force a guidebook to becoming rich—if the young entrant will only take the time to read the manual. Alas, few will take that time—and they'll suffer for it.

Capitalism is like the ancient feudal system, except now the serfs and peasants can work and save up to own the castle and estates. Or . . . they can lie on their couches, smoke weed, and pretend they have legitimate obstacles to success in a "rigged system"—that is, they can instead do nothing and stay serfs. Life can be faced by moaning and complaining or it can be faced by study, work, optimism, and faith in the free capitalist system. Guess which side gets to live a happier life?

FREE WILL OF THE INDIVIDUAL

What is capitalism? There are many definitions, but the one that applies to us in twenty-first-century America is this: capitalism is a system in which economic decisions are made by individuals voluntarily on the basis of whether they think the decisions will help or harm them financially.

It's a scheme whereby the key factor in the production and distribution of goods and services is the deployment of money—or capital—from private sources to private users of the funds, with those decisions made by private entities. In capitalism, decisions are not enforced based on the whim of the government but by the free will of the individual as such or as part of a group—often a much larger group.

In this system of free market democratic capitalism, the means of production, distribution, and communication are usually (but not always) owned through possession of shares of stock in publicly owned corporations. These are entities that gather investment funds and do all the hard work of running the investments but then have limited liability if things go bad. The liability of the owner is limited to how much money he or she put in. There is generally no liability beyond that for borrowings or any other obligations of the corporation. In Europe, these vehicles are often called "LLCs" (limited liability corporations). This part of free market capitalism—limiting the liability and the downside of the investors and yet having no upside limits—is a magnificent lure for investors. In fact, it was not until the eighteenth century, when the limited liability feature came into being, that corporate investing skyrocketed.

STOCKS AND THE OWNERSHIP CLASS

Stocks that evidence property in a corporation can be owned in small amounts by an individual. Anyone can buy a few hundred dollars' worth of ownership in Ford Motor Company. Or stocks can be owned in extremely large amounts by fantastically wealthy individuals, such as Bill Gates of Microsoft and Warren Buffett of Berkshire Hathaway—of whom there will be much more to come.

But more often, ownership of the public shares of a corporation that owns important chunks of production and distribution is in the hands of aggregations of people. These would be the beneficiaries of the pension funds of large corporations and of unions of factory workers, or teachers, or even Hollywood screenwriters. Or they can be investors in investment vehicles such as "mutual funds," "index funds," or "exchange-traded funds," in which great volumes of stock are put together under some guiding principle of investment and then sold to investors of all sizes.

The main point is that private individuals and entities own the means of production and distribution, and anyone can be part of this ownership class. The government is *not* the owner.

REWARDS OF GOOD ECONOMIC DECISIONS

In this system, enormous rewards flow to persons who have made good economic decisions. If they have made good economic decisions over long periods of time, the rewards can be startlingly large.

Wrong decisions are not punished by terms in prison camps or by firing squads as in government-run dictatorial states. Instead, they are punished by a lack of economic advancement or by being fired. That's much better than being fired upon.

In free market capitalism, the major means of production—factories, formulas, farmland, coal mines, oil fields, stores, airplanes, railroads—are owned by private individuals, not by the government. So are the smaller means of production and distribution—car dealerships, florists, restaurants, clothing stores, and boutique manufacturers.

To be sure, the government still owns immense resources, especially in terms of land and the minerals that lie under the land and in terms of bridges, tunnels, airports, and licenses. The government also has great power to regulate the private sector and even sometimes to confiscate it. But this power is subject to counterattack in the courts and even in regulatory agencies.

To give you an example, almost every weeknight I watch my dear pal, Jimmy Kimmel, on ABC. He makes me laugh and brightens my day. He's a private person. His production company is private; the networks that distribute his show are private. There is no "Department of TV Comedy" on Constitution Avenue in the District of Columbia. It's all done privately and works superbly well—although in recent years, some government officials have been funnier than anything even Jimmy Kimmel could dream up. You and I can easily become owners of the Walt Disney Company, which owns ABC. In that way, in a very small manner, we own a huge factory that manufactures laughter and relaxation. We can also own ownership stock in the companies that send out Jimmy Kimmel on cable and in the companies that make the TV sets and the popcorn we eat while we watch TV.

For you, readers, most of whom I assume to be young, the key point is that there is more or less free access to any person in America who has saved a few shekels to become an investor in these private resources. If these purchase decisions are made sensibly—not brilliantly, but fairly sensibly—and if they are made consistently, the investor can and will become a well-heeled man or woman. In fact, this investor is pretty much guaranteed to get rich.

This means, of course, a greatly enhanced standard of life and opportunities to travel and to get one's children better education, better medical care, and better, safer cars. Being part of the capitalist machine makes a family more independent too. That family need not fear that if a mean-spirited boss fires the breadwinner, the whole family will go down in flames.

Owning part of the means of production, however small that ownership share starts, erects a fortress around the family. They can pay their bills and keep their lives comfortable even when others like them who have been fired—but who are lacking in property—are in terror. Property, especially the property that is part of the machinery of what produces the national product of America, is safety. If you do it right, it produces income whether you are at work or not.

With capital and the income from it, you can maintain your health, your morale, and yourself in ways that persons without property cannot.

In sum, capitalism is a thing of beauty. It's not the same as long ago when heredity and physical strength determined who would have capital. In the past, you had to inherit land or factories to have capital. Women were largely excluded from owning capital; accidents of birth decided everything. This is still true in many parts of the world.

That's all changed now thanks to free market, democratic capitalism. Anyone can be a capitalist—and should be. All it takes is a little bit of knowledge and an even smaller amount of action.

In today's world, to coin a phrase, any man (or woman) can be a king (or queen).

CHAPTER TWO

HOW I LEARNED TO STOP WORRYING
AND LOVE CAPITALISM

I finally know what distinguishes man from the other beasts: financial worry.

—Jules Renard

Let's start this part of our story by talking about men and women perhaps a bit older than most of you readers. Let's assume we're talking about your parents or grandparents.

They have serious fears, largely because they did not understand what free market, democratic capitalism is.

It's a little more graphic than that. A nightmare is haunting America: the fear of personal financial disaster. The fear is that although the middle-class American is sitting in front of his TV watching three hundred channels about zombies and dope addict Hollywood stars, or planning her next trip to the Bahamas, or wondering where his son might get into college, some horrible day down the road, he or she will simply run out of money. This can happen, and it does. Every year, roughly one million Americans go into bankruptcy, and many more than that are seriously delinquent on payments on credit cards or other loans.

Throughout the land—and perhaps even within your own family—there is the fear that although today we are the ones driving down Sunset Boulevard or Main Street in our air-conditioned Lexuses and listening to music on stereos that billionaires would have envied ten years ago, someday we will be one of those guys dumpster diving right next to us at the stoplight.

THE REALITY OF FINANCIAL COLLAPSE

This fear takes on a concrete aspect when we see so many homeless Americans. We are afraid of terrorism, of course, and we should be. But we don't see victims of terrorism all around us every day as if we were in Baghdad or Fallujah. We're afraid of nuclear war, but we've become numb to that. The Cuban missile crisis was a long time ago, and the Iranian bomb is still in the future. The North Koreans are awakening us, but not enough. The day Seattle goes up in flames, it won't be a sanctuary city any longer. But that's in the future.

Yet almost every one of us, if we are alive and alert, sees the homeless frequently, and once in a while, we might even recognize the facial features of someone we know. Even if we do not come up against actual homelessness, almost every one of us knows someone who once had comfortable middle-class or upper-middle-class or even upper-class status and is now in dire straits, living on tiny social security checks and cadging loans from us that will never be repaid. We all know people who used to throw the bums a dime in their prime or toss ten-dollar bills to valets and bell boys and who now consider it a luxury to get Domino's pizza. (In fact, Domino's really is awfully good, but that's sort of beside the point.) We all know people who look at statements from their brokers or from their banks and look at their most recent cancelled bank checks and can count the months until they run out of money.

It happened to many of my best friends; people who once lived with confidence, in authentic luxury, are now reduced to actual terror or prolonged despair. In any given week, I hear from several of them. They almost always want money, and if the requestor is genuinely a lifelong friend, I usually give it. (This, by the way, is only one of my many stupid and self-destructive habits. I pray it does not kill me.) Or they want a financial miracle from me in the form of advice that can turn their lives around on a dime. But they are in their sixties or seventies. I am not a miracle worker, and if a man with several dependents is really close to broke, I simply lack the wherewithal to pull him and those of his like out of the ditch. I wish these people had come to me thirty years ago and asked the same questions. I wish I had asked myself the same questions forty years ago.

And again, to go back to the grimmest example, although few of the homeless were once solidly middle class, just seeing human beings with two arms and two legs like most of us living in rags and shuffling down alleys is terrifying: *It happened to them. Who's to say it won't happen to us?*

And yet again (and it's worth scaring you with this a few times), in fact, in real life, people's financial lives do collapse. We usually see this as something less than homelessness. But we see a drastic change in lifestyle—from suburban four-bedroom manse in Hancock Park to studio apartment in Van Nuys—all too often. And we as sentient human beings worry about it. We would be mistaken *not* to worry about it. And we don't just worry about it; we're in serious fear about it. Not all of us, but enough of us to want to do something.

LIFE HAPPENS

We don't have to do anything really wrong for this kind of catastrophe to happen. We don't have to be caught in a scandal or a crime. No need for an accident or an illness. No need even for a divorce. It's just part of the progression of life for incomes to go up and then down. This is not a disgrace. It isn't a mark of shame. It's life. It is so much a part of life that Milton Friedman, the megagenius economist whom I often cite, wrote about it as a basic tenet of life.

We will tend to ("will tend to," not "are required to") spend all of what we earn. We will tend not to have enough for a comfortable retirement. Again, this will not happen to everyone, but it will happen to tens of millions of us.

Incomes rise and fall, and jobs are found and lost, and if we do not make provisions for this virtual inevitability, we will suffer. We don't want it to happen to us. It's not pretty.

Even more inevitably, we are rightly in serious fear—actual terror—about what happens when we are past our prime. Again, what the devil happens to us when we are put out to pasture and no longer have a regular paycheck? What happens when we are locked into that hellish world where we have grown used to spending a certain amount on cars and mortgages and supporting our children and then suddenly the x factor necessary to support that lifestyle, that x factor that was coming in like clockwork for decades, becomes 10 percent of x? What happens when we become like Wile E. Coyote and run off a cliff, our legs still pedaling in midair, and suddenly look down to see there's nothing supporting us and an anvil is about to fall on our heads just after we hit the ground?

(This, again, was a part of what Friedman won the Nobel Prize for—the lifetime consumption function.)

NO PLAN = NO MONEY

To illustrate, here in Hollywood, there's a classic "joke" about TV writers and their employers: "They pay us $5,000 a week until we need $5,000 a week to live on, and then they fire us." It's called "The Velvet Alley," and it's all too real. Roughly

60 percent of boomers are seriously worried about this fate and believe they have not prepared adequately for it. I queried a number of financial planners who said that in their experience, the actual percentage is higher. I've been told almost everyone (except those who are delusional on one end of the scale or who live with the utmost rigor and good sense on the other) is in fear.

True, the majority of boomers have at least some financial plan. It's a small majority, and it excludes tens of millions. It might be inadequate, but at least there's a plan. That's positive luxury compared with what awaits the ones without a plan—and that includes many millennials. (The millennials, to be sure, are young enough to do something about it, and I hope they will. But the cards are stacked against them in many ways, including home ownership and pensions, so they have to play a clever hand to turn the trick of retirement. Boomers often had the great cards of a rising real estate market, owning their own homes, which they bought when real estate was affordable to those starting out in their work lives, and the long-discarded defined benefit pension plan. Those cards are unlikely to be dealt out again. What's in the cards for the boomers as yet without a plan and for the millennials—well, that's what this slender book is about.)

Roughly 80 percent of millennials—some of whom are now in their late thirties by some definitions—have no plan at all. They are not saving any meaningful sums for retirement. In fact, they are not saving at all. They have no plan, and they have no planners. And they have no money. And they know very little about finance and money. This is not a formula for sleeping well at night.

Or look at it from another angle (a genuine vertiginous occlusion, to use one of the fabulous phrases of the great writer Joan Didion): more than half of American families could not come up with *five hundred dollars* on the spot for an emergency. Back it up from there and try to think how many have enough saved to cover their salaries if there is another Great Depression (a highly doubtful prospect), or when they leave the labor force, kicking and screaming (a virtual certainty), or when they get laid off because robots can do their jobs. And those robots are getting smarter every day.

But it's not all about fear. There are people who do have plans and have yachts and tanned faces and confident smiles. They're in the ads for investment planning firms. There are not many of them in real life. They're actors or models in front of cameras, with makeup artists to make them look great. And often a dog or a horse—a sure sign of stability.

But let's get back to reality. In this glorious America, there are simply not enough who actually do have a plan of any kind at all or even any meaningful idea of how the system works to get them to that TV commercial beach and that magazine and that sailboat or anything even a little like it.

Just to hit you over the head with this again in numbers, the average Americans nearing retirement say they need roughly $50,000 a year to live on. But they have savings sufficient to generate less than 20 percent of that. Yes, they will have some small sums from Social Security, which will make things better. Yes, some will have been able to serve in the public sector for long periods and accrue those gorgeous public sector pensions that they suck out of the jugulars of the taxpayers. (By the way, that won't last. Taxpayers will not forever suffer being impoverished so that civil servants can retire in comfort.) But a huge number will experience a spectacular shortfall after they retire. Too many will simply run out of money except to live at a depressingly modest level. Buttered toast happens to be one of my wife's and my favorite meals, but to eat it every day would be a bad feeling.

CONFIDENT, LUSTY, AND CHEERFUL

My goal is to help create a few million more of those confident, lusty, cheerful people, obviously enjoying themselves in the advertisements and commercials until the final curtain sets—not just to create them on TV or on a magazine page, but to create them in real life.

There is a way to do it. It involves having some contact with the reality of our system, the capitalist system, our frequently reviled but beautiful reality. And it involves having a plan.

The greatest genius about money since Adam Smith, Warren E. Buffett, has said, "An idiot with a plan can beat a genius without a plan." My El Dorado, the gilded city of my dreams, is to give you that plan.

It's a really basic plan. As I like to say, "No one is too stupid to get it, but some are too smart."

CHAPTER THREE

THE PRE-DAD CLASS

Someone is sitting in the shade today because someone planted a tree a long time ago.

—Warren Buffett

To continue with this little volume, some words about its genesis are in order. They basically tell the whole story.

I could start anywhere, but for now, let's start with my brilliant sister, Rachel Epstein of Brooklyn, New York. She is a spectacularly well-educated woman, a writer, housewife, and mother, and she has been a fundraiser for various causes most of her adult life.

One day, say twenty-five years ago, she returned from a fund-gathering party in a ritzy New Jersey suburb of New York to meet me for lunch. The organizers had raked in tons of money. I asked her if the women at the event (it was a women's event, specifically a housewives' event) were the wives of doctors and lawyers or business executives. "No," she said. "Much better than that. Their husbands are owners of businesses. Usually they inherited those businesses from their parents or their grandparents. There's such a thing as being premed and such a thing as being prelaw, and those are fine," said my smart sister. "But the best of all is 'pre-dad.'"

"Yes, yes, yes," thought your humble scribe. "That's exactly right. Nothing can compare with owning a business where you start out at birth owning a stream of income that comes gushing at you. You don't have to work your way up. You don't have to put in long hours. There is no risk that you won't wind up on top. Money is yours from the capital that your parents or in-laws or other ancestors laid up for you long ago. What could be better than owning a business where you don't even have to show up? Your employees show up and do the heavy lifting and you get the profits! That sounds great." So ran my febrile thoughts.

Now, today this story might be different. There would be many charity events where women were the business owners either by their own exertions or by inheritance. But the principle would be the same. Fortunate is the man or woman who owns a business that tosses off money without him or her having to go into an office or onto a factory floor. "God bless the child that's got his own," as the saying goes.

NOT EVERYONE IS AN ENTREPRENEUR

But how do we do that? There are only a few thousand large family-owned businesses in this country, and there are 335 million of us Americans. Even if you took a smaller business—such as owning a string of dry cleaners in the suburbs of Buffalo, which would generate a lot of money—it takes a special, super-high-energy, self-starting kind of guy or gal to organize and run a business. It's exhausting. It's dicey. It involves large risks of failure. To inherit it once it's already up and running is far better.

Americans are an unusually entrepreneurial race. But if we are not born entrepreneurs, and if our forebears weren't, what can we do? "Look on in envy at those who are," I guessed as I talked to my sister. Otherwise, we are just plain out of luck. We'll have to be wage slaves all our lives. Boohoo. It would be nice to own a business, but maybe we're just not the type to own our own business. Sad.

Perhaps the genesis of this little tome started there, with my envy of the pre-dad class. Or maybe just with the notion that there is such a thing as owning a business that's tossing off scads of cash, and it would be damned nice to be one of those owners. More than nice—the stuff that dreams are made of.

BUYING A PIECE OF SUCCESS

Or we could start with another incident. Back in 1973–74, after the Yom Kippur War in the Middle East, the Arab oil exporters punished America for its support of Israel, which had again soundly beaten the Arabs on the battlefield.

The Arabs slapped an oil embargo on the United States. At that time, the United States was heavily dependent on Middle Eastern oil. This was before the miracles of domestic U.S. shale and fracking. The U.S. consumer in 1973–74 saw an immense rise in the price of oil at the pump. But it takes an ill wind to blow no one any good, and there was a fine wind blowing for large oil companies.

Some of the U.S. oil producers had vast holdings of oil reserves in the United States. They had acquired those holdings when oil was at fifty cents to the barrel or less. A barrel is forty-two gallons. Suddenly, back in '73, oil was going for thirty dollars a barrel or more. The profits to the oil companies from these old fields were fantastic.

I looked at this scene with the normal human reaction: envy. I said to my father at this time, "These profits are just obscene."

My father heaved a weary economist's sigh and asked, "Do you really think the profits are obscene, and do you think they'll last?"

"Yes and yes," said I.

"Well," rejoined my brilliant old dad, "you have some money. Why don't you buy some stock in the big oil companies?"

I scoffed at first, as smart-aleck kids do it their genuinely smart parents. But when I thought about it, I realized my father was right. I didn't have a plot of land in West Texas where I could drill for oil, see it explode up from the ground, and then sell it for millions. I didn't have a network of natural-gas-gathering hardware all over Oklahoma or Arkansas. But I could buy an infinitesimal piece of an oil major. That was, in a tiny way, the same as if I did own a supersmall oil field. I would still get money from rises in the price of oil. I would be in the oil business. I liked it and actually did buy a few pennies' worth of some oil companies, and they did well.

That was my first inkling that I could, through the stock market, be—in a microscopic way—"pre-dad."

I could own my own teeny-tiny business, as if my ancestors had been in the oil trade.

I should have seen it much sooner. Through the generosity of friends and relatives and my own savings from summer jobs, I had a small amount of savings, and some of these were in stock. But I saw the corporations in which I owned stock as faraway nations whose high pooh-bahs lived lives of power and luxury and whose stock sometimes went up and sometimes went down.

I saw the stocks I owned as being valuable almost entirely through what Mr. Buffett calls "price action." I did not see them as businesses in which I was an extremely junior partner. This silly idea, that I owned a number on a Quotron (an early precursor to the now ubiquitous electronic ticker) and nothing physical, was borne in on me by the news media, which dwelt endlessly on day-by-day moves in the stock market and not on the fundamental earnings of companies. The idea that I owned basically nothing but a glimpse at the financial pages was underscored by the (totally correct) reporting on the misconduct of corporate executives and their depredations against their holders.

The media rarely, if ever, discussed giant corporations like Douglas, one of my first investments, as an adventure in ownership of high-end aerospace. The company might as well have been on another planet. I was just owning a day-by-day price and a quarterly dividend.

This was an extremely superficial analysis, to put it mildly. Owning stock was not just owning a note in small type in a newspaper about what the stock was selling for. It was owning a part of a business.

WIDOWS AND ORPHANS

I should have seen this at least when I was a college student at Columbia. My first economics teacher, the great C. Lowell Harriss, always urged us when thinking about corporations to imagine that all their owners were widows and orphans. That implied some duty of good conduct by corporate officers toward us owners, as small as we were. While there would be evil managers who disdained us stockholders and stole from us, more of them were running a good business that we could be part owners of. This sounds simple, but to this day, the great majority of young people and even old people whom I meet do not understand it. And back then, when LBJ was president, I surely didn't get it. To me, corporations' stocks were merely bets to be placed on the roulette velvet of life. If I hit a number, it was good, and if I didn't, I was out of there. I didn't get that I owned a piece of a business: machinery, buildings, land, patents, workers. The interaction of these to make money over time was the key thing I owned. But I didn't get it.

PRIDE OF OWNERSHIP

And I surely should have gotten it in the mid-1970s when I moved to Los Angeles. It was then that my smart literary agent told me to buy a book called *Walker's Manual of Western Corporations* and see if there were any local Southern California companies whose stock looked attractive. I read the book and actually lit upon one called the Los Angeles Athletic Club Company, or LAACO. It was a recreational club or clubs and also a holding company for real estate in the greater Southland of California. It was old California money. As far as I could tell by reading its entry in *Walker's*, it sat on a combination of cash and real estate that was worth a hefty premium over the price at which the stock was selling.

LAACO had been majority owned and run by a prominent local family, the Hathaways, for roughly eighty years when I found it. Its shares traded rarely, but again, their price seemed to be a small fraction of what the assets of the company were worth.

Plus, as most of the shareholders were related to one another, there was reason to believe the company would be managed on the up-and-up to avoid family disharmony and because by nature the Hathaways were fine people. I bought some, and I wish I had bought more.

LAACO turned out to be the first company whose shares I could see up close. I could see that it genuinely was primarily managed in the interests of the owners and only minimally in the interests of the managers. And I was a member of this small "family" of shareholders almost as if I were a Hathaway cousin. The small economies, the thrifty way the Athletic Club was run, were for my benefit.

This was a revelation: I actually was, in a tiny way, the owner of an extremely well-run recreation and real estate holding company in the then booming LA area. (It's booming again now.) The stock went up, and it even paid a sizeable dividend. So there, every quarter, in the mail, was tangible evidence that LAACO was making money and I was getting some.

Plus, I had the pleasure of meeting the higher-ups at LAACO in person. They were polite, stunningly smart about real estate, and thoroughly pleasant people. By just a small investment, I had become "pre-dad" in real estate. I had become the partner of the brilliant, shining, successful Hathaways of

Los Angeles. Again, in a sense, I was a child of the Hathaways, and they certainly treated me that way.

Alas, SoCal is subject to wild swings in real estate valuations. This moved the stock in LAACO and scared me to the point that I thought I had better diversify somewhat away from Southern California property. I sold a small amount of LAACO. Mistake! Still, I kept a lot of what I owned. The dividends were paid like clockwork, and I was genuinely "pre-dad" on the petri dish of investing and money.

So there really were corporations whose management made us stockholders' partners. Some years later, LAACO did in fact shift to a partnership form of ownership, and its partnership interests are publicly traded. They trade rarely, but look them up and decide for yourself. The ticker is LAACZ.

That same agent who led me to LAACO also told me about his favorite stock, something I had never heard of called "Berkshire Hathaway." He said it was a stock one must never sell. I bought some and then handled it in almost exactly the wrong way. (By the way, it's pure coincidence that two of the absolute best investments of my life involve the name "Hathaway." There is no connection at all between the two entities except that I write about them occasionally.)

THE GENIUS OF WARREN BUFFETT

Berkshire Hathaway was run in majority measure by the supernova genius Warren Buffett, whom I mentioned above. He was a megastar at investing and in finding great uses for the stockholders' money. "Genius" doesn't even take it anywhere near far enough. He was uniquely talented at investing.

He had started Berkshire Hathaway (BRK) as an investment partnership in about 1967. His first few investments were not wild successes. But soon he was hitting one home run after another. An investment of a few dollars in BRK had become worth thousands of dollars. He had a true gift for investing such as had never been seen before, at least not by most mortals.

In large part, this came from his brilliance at insurance. He had bought a number of insurance companies. All of these used what is called "float." That's the money the premium payors had paid in, which the insurer got to hold onto until it was paid in death benefits (for instance) or car accident payments (for another instance).

Most insurers used this "float" to buy ultrasafe investments like Treasury bonds. But Buffett used a large part of his "float" (I think I'll stop putting it in quotes now) to buy stock in companies he liked. His gift for this was fantastic. Soon, he was manufacturing money. His stock, which had started trading in 1967 at about $12, was, when I came upon it in about 1978, at about $1,000.

I bought a small amount and started to get his famous stockholders' letters. The letters offered brilliant insights into how the world works. But one point was made over and over by Mr. Warren Buffett (*Berkshire Hathaway Shareholder Letters, 1965–2014):* Mr. Buffett and his cohost, Charlie Munger, veep of BRK, regarded us stockholders as their partners. They wanted us to hold onto their stock forever, experience its growth, and not trade in and out of it.

They used the same principle in their own stock buying. They bought companies in which they wanted to be partners—or owners of the whole darned thing—forever, not just for a quick profit.

Frankly, I did not find it convincing. The news was made by people who did trade in and out for a quick buck. Could Mr. Buffett really be that much of a pal and brother to us little stockholders? It was hard to believe that it was anything beyond salesmanship.

Besides, the major financial magazines, including my own beloved *Barron's*, for whom I wrote long pieces about financial fraud, frequently were bearish on BRK. They had all kinds of reasons why it was overpriced and bound to crash. Plus, the man who had suggested it to me said he was selling and I should sell too.

I did sell some, and I lived to regret it bitterly.

It turned out that Mr. Buffett was telling us the truth. He really was striving mightily to create a moneymaking juggernaut for us small stockholders. For a salary of close to zero, he was allowing us little guys and gals to ride on his gravy train. We got to be participants in the supreme moneymaking machinery of BRK, and over time, it became a miracle. As I said earlier, I am not a miracle worker. Warren Buffett is.

VALUE INVESTING

Very importantly, while BRK definitely made money from the "price action" of its stockholdings, Mr. Buffett endlessly reminded us that he wanted us to think as owners of operating businesses and to get our earnings and growth in book value and not only speculative gains.

I had so little of BRK that it did not make me a rich man. But it did tell me that I should have been far more trusting of Mr. Buffett. And it also let me know that I was now allowed to be "pre-dad" in the amazing way that Warren E. Buffett (supreme genius of all time where money is concerned and, frankly, a genius about everything, the ultragodfather of investing) was *my dad!* He's too young to be my real dad, but you get the point.

So now I had the Hathaways of the Los Angeles Athletic Club Company as my dads. And I had the ultimate Hathaway, Warren, as my ultimate dad.

Still, while it made me mildly well-to-do, it did not make me rich, and my eyes were still not fully seeing the light.

In my pitiful, self-pitying way, I was missing a far bigger picture. I'll try to explain it now.

BE A ROCK

Here it is in a nutshell. In the free market capitalist society, a highly disproportionate amount of the good things in life accrue to those who have financial capital. Human beings who have nothing to sell but their labor usually—not always—are the ones waiting on the tables and cracking open the lobsters.

The men and women feasting at the tables were the capitalists. The men and women who had only their strong backs and weak or strong minds to rely on were just chaff in the wind of life. Those who were anchored to capital were strong and fixed in comfortable spots overlooking the ocean.

You already knew that, right? You know that it's great to have money. Life is entirely different—happier, more secure, more peaceful—when you have money. You are a whole new species as a rich or at least well-off person if you have money. You look different. You hold yourself differently. You are a rock instead of a grain of sand. A man or woman with capital is a happier man. That may not be true when you're in college or in your twenties and your blood pressure is good and you can have all the romance you want. Then money is a second-order good. But when you get into your thirties and forties, it's a whole different world. Money becomes extremely important in every way—especially in the way you see yourself.

You're a better you if you have money. It's that basic.

You already knew that, right? Of course you did. But what you don't know, or at least what many of you don't know, is that it just takes that great invention—*a plan*—to get on the right side of history and to be the best thing you can be in the capitalist society: a capitalist. If Mr. Buffett and the Hathaways of Los Angeles could carry me on their backs, I could get there.

But how? My dad was a genuinely great man, a genius economist and advisor to presidents and corporate chieftains. But he did not have a business to leave to me. Maybe he would leave me money someday, but that day was so unthinkably horrible that I didn't think about it. How would I be pre-dad?

I could get there through the miracle of the public corporation. It was and is a fantastic fountain of good things for us little people. What the Hathaways of LAACO and Warren Buffett of Berkshire Hathaway had to teach me was that they were the path. They're the path for everyone who cares to get to the destination of financial security. They were the road map to getting in on the billowing fountain of money being thrown off by the capitalist system—money that irrigated the best crop in the world, prosperity.

THERE IT IS, TAKE IT ALL!

Long ago, my beloved Los Angeles was greatly limited in what it could be by a shortage of water. After all, we are in a desert and next to a salty ocean. But there was a powerful river north of Los Angeles, the Owens River, that ran into a lake called Lake Owens. The city engineer of Los Angeles, William Mulholland, craftily, through the city, but under many phony names, bought up the riparian rights for most of the lake. He then built a canal and had the water sent down to Los Angeles in a mighty aqueduct. When he pressed the buttons that dynamited a dam and let the water flood into the water mains of Los Angeles, he reportedly said, "There it is. Take it!"

That's the way to feel about the money to be had from ownership in public corporations. They are reviled, cursed at, spat upon, and yet, and yet, "There it is. Take it!" Now, true, Lake Owens is a lot smaller now. But that's another story (told in the great movie *Chinatown*). The real story is that it's raining money—over long periods, not at all quarter by quarter or year by year—from corporate earnings, and if you don't put out your bucket, you are making a mistake.

I owe my fervor on this subject in large measure to a charming woman senator from Massachusetts, Elizabeth Warren, a teacher at Harvard Law School. With exactly the opposite intention, she made clear why investing in corporations is such a great life plan.

In the 2012 election, she gave an emotional speech to the Democratic National Convention delegates. In her speech, she excoriated the Republicans. The GOP, she said, was the party of "the corporations." She said it with rage coming out of her mouth. Corporations are not human, she insisted. Corporations don't have feelings. "Corporations don't cry," said Professor Warren. And it was then and there I realized that young Americans were being fed a diet of pure nonsense about how the world works. If young Americans could just eat their way through that bologna, they could get to some really tasty gnawing.

THE HUMAN CONNECTION

The point is, of course, that Senator Elizabeth Warren had it totally wrong. Corporations are organizations of men and women who work to produce goods and services. Those people have emotions. Those people feel exhilaration and also feel fear and pain and loss. Corporations are owned largely by men and women who are saving for their retirement. Those people feel joy and pain and sorrow and most certainly do cry. Corporations are owned largely by university endowments. They use some of the income from those endowments to pay professors like Mrs. Warren many thousands of dollars *per hour* of classroom time. If that's not enough to make people cry. . . .

Corporations sell their goods and services to human beings. Those are flesh-and-blood people too. People buying food, houses, medicine, tickets to travel to see their widowed parents. Those people have every bit as much of human feeling—all of those people, the owners, the workers, the managers, the customers—as Mrs. Warren's students at Harvard Law School. Or as Mrs. Warren herself.

But it goes way beyond that. The corporation is a miraculous invention that basically allows farmers and shopkeepers and taxi drivers and lawyers who cannot start a business to be the owners of a business—without the endless liability that you or I could have if we started our own toy business or Internet business or space exploration business. In fact, you will notice that some corporations have their name and then the letters *LLC* after the name.

As you learned in Chapter One, LLC stands for "limited liability corporation." That means you can own shares in a corporation—ownership—without facing any kind of liability at all beyond the loss of your investment if your company tanks. This, as any owner of any family business that's gone bust can tell you, is perfection.

Mrs. Warren, undoubtedly a fine human being, got it absolutely wrong about corporations. As legal entities, they are morally neutral. They are just aggregations of people, some of whom will be evil and most of whom will not be evil. There are a lot of greedy people in corporations, but then there are a lot of greedy people everywhere. It would be awfully difficult to prove that there are more greedy people per thousand at a corporation than in a government office. Yes, the top dogs at corporations will be far more aggressive than bureaucrats. They will be far more likely to take risks and push the envelope. But would they in their heart of hearts love money more than the average Cuban secret policeman (a character I am guessing Mrs. Warren admires)?

That would be extremely difficult to prove. Corporations are just people, and people, as my super-braino sister says, "Are not such hot items."

Corporations are just ways to allow the little guy or woman to own a business, to be "pre-dad" without facing bottomless liability. In fact, in this way, corporations are *not* morally neutral. They are better than morally neutral. They are a historically uniquely great way for the little guy to amass capital—to join in the "pre-dad" club and the ultragreat and utterly nondiscriminatory capitalists' club. That's the club you want to be in. It has the best food and the cleanest restrooms.

Another little note: Corporations do not start or wage wars, at least not large wars. Corporations do not round up Jews and put them in cattle cars and send them to be gassed. Corporations do not bomb Pearl Harbor. Corporations do not kill one-third of all Cambodians in the name of equality. Corporations do not starve to death millions of Ukrainians in the name of creating "the new Soviet man." Corporations do not kill one hundred million of the world's most brilliant people, the Chinese, to create Mao's slave state. Corporations do not run the most evil country in the world, North Korea, and work men and women to death while raping the women and then keeping the children of these rapes as slaves for life. Probably the worst thing the modern corporation does is oil spills. Those are accidents. Genocide is done by governments and academic lunatics and ideologues looking for equality and a racial superstate—and they do it on purpose.

THE FREEWAY TO FINANCIAL HAPPINESS

But let's get back to investing: there is a stunning, simple beauty about corporations and their utility. They are the freeway to financial happiness if you are driving in the correct lane. Over long periods of time, if you own the stock in corporations correctly, you get to participate in the entire growth of the U.S. economy (or the world economy, or the

Japanese economy, or what have you) and to allow its growth to propel you to reach the great nirvana: financial security. You get to be "pre-dad" for the whole country (or even for the whole world). Your "Dad" (or "Mom," if you will) is all the large public corporations in America (or anywhere in the world, but we'll confine our observations mostly to the corporations in America).

The great French architect Le Corbusier famously said, "A house is a machine for living." Just so, a corporation is a machine for making money. And for making some considerable measure of comfort in your old age. And there are now ways, and not just a few ways, in which you can be "pre-dad" for the whole capitalist world.

Just file this away for your future. I know I just said it, but a corporation is a machine for making money for its owners. Here's how to be one of them in the most effective, inexpensive way possible (that I know of).

CHAPTER FOUR

A GLORY OF LIFE

Do what you love, the money will follow.

—Marsha Sinetar

First, you have to have some money to invest. There is an old Steve Martin skit from the early years of *Saturday Night Live*—when it was actually funny. That was a long time ago. Steve Martin stands on the stage and says, "Want to know how to make a million dollars and never pay any tax?" He pauses for a moment and then says, "First, get a million dollars! Then don't pay any tax. When the IRS agent comes to the door, just say, 'I *forgot*!'"

This is a joke, but there is also a big lesson here.

Let's go back to the starting point: where do we get that million dollars?

For most of us, we cannot just start with a letter to Mom and Pop asking for a million dollars. We have to earn some money and save a decent chunk of it. How do we do that? How, in a world that endlessly tells you to buy, do you save?

You get it into your noggin that if you don't save, you will suffer terribly later on in life.

That's hard to do. It's similar to giving up drinking or smoking.

It feels great to spend money. My son refers to it as "retail therapy," and he's right. Buying something for yourself or someone else can change your mood; just going to your favorite website, signing on, and buying something makes you feel better.

Is it the feeling that someone is giving us a present? Is it the feeling of power we have over the store clerk? Is it the shock of knowing that we own something new—or used? Is it a feeling of being fortified in some way? We don't really know. We just know it feels great to buy goods and services.

Alas, we also know that—for most of us—it does not feel so great to get the MasterCard, or Visa, or American Express credit card bills. That's when we feel weak, vulnerable, exposed—mortal.

The bigger the bills, the worse we feel. That's just human nature.

The pain is especially great if our bills are large in proportion to how much we earn, or how much we have in the bank, or our assets generally.

BILLS, BILLS, BILLS

If I may, I'll tell a little story. When I first moved to Hollywood, I was making far more money than I had ever made before. It was tiny by the standards of the truly successful, but it was more than I had ever made before.

My spending was still under control, as it had been when I was a journalist in New York City and even buying Chinese takeout was a special treat.

Thus when I got my bills, I laughed and smiled as I paid them. They were a joke compared to what I was making in those palmy days of 1976–77.

Time passed. I found myself spending vastly more and yet earning more still. And then, *boom*, my earnings fell dramatically. The bills were still coming in, bigger than ever. Now, it got to be a scary thing to open those bills. That was one of the many motivations I had to greatly accelerate my savings program; I simply had to harmonize my spending and my earning.

If I ever had a year when I earned far more than I spent—or even a little more—and had saved some of it, I was a happy guy. If I saw my savings going down, I felt like a person watching a car's falling fuel level indicator when he's far from a gas station. I was terrified.

Again, this is human nature. We feel great when we spend, but we feel terrible to be behind the eight ball financially. This is—and always has been—a fact of our poor, vulnerable human lives.

We must allow it to teach us. We must save.

And how do we get to the point where we not only spend less but earn more? *We work.* We get the maximum amount of education we possibly can. We get the taxpayers and the donors to the schools we attend to pick up as much of the tab as possible.

In today's world, this turns out to be a license to steal. There are grants, loans, and fellowships of all kinds to help pay for college and graduate school.

IMPORTANCE OF EDUCATION

Now that students have become such an immense part of the voting population, they are using that power in many different ways to get subsidized schooling.

One of the greatest geniuses of economics, the superbraino of the University of Chicago, Frank Knight, had a commandment: "Take advantage of all subsidies." The taxpayers and wealthy people (and corporations) subsidize education in thousands of ways.

Take advantage of it.

There is a clear, unequivocal, if generalized, connection between the amount of education that a man or woman achieves and the amount he or she earns. This is not a one-to-one connection in every case, to be sure. A college or graduate school degree is not a pipeline to Scrooge McDuck's cash-filled swimming pool (one of the favorite images of my dear pal Phil DeMuth, master investment manager). A respected electrician with only high school and apprenticeship learning can and does earn more than a Princeton-graduated teacher of poetry at an elite, big-city, private day school. A high school grad who knows how to plumb a house and hires several journeyman plumbers to work under him in Beverly Hills can and will earn more than a Columbia University PhD in French literature who teaches at a community college.

My wife and I have a house in Rancho Mirage with many windows. Those windows get dust blown onto them. They need to be cleaned several times a year.

A man or woman with no education to speak of can hire low-level workers at minimum wage—say, roughly $11 per hour—to clean the windows. The work takes two men one day of eight hours of labor. The men get paid roughly $90 each, or $180 total. The Windex and paper towels are another $50 at most. The home owner gets charged about $500. The entrepreneur has paid out roughly $230 and has made roughly $270. His workers can do three different houses in a day, and he does not have to clean one window.

By my reckoning, he's making about $800 a day, or about $4,000 a week, with very little training needed but, to be sure, with a lot of energy and drive required.

The point is that there are ways to make money without much education or initial capital. It's not only B-school grads who make money.

Mind you, I am not advising that you own a window washing company (although, why not?). I am merely pointing out that there are many ways to make money. But in general and as a rule, college grads earn far more than high school grads. The difference is stunning—the typical college grad makes about double what a high school grad makes. High school dropouts are in even more trouble. Yes, they can become drug dealers, but that's not much of a life.

College grads who go on to professional schools will earn far more than the usual liberal arts college grad. This is well known. The following data are from a recent study conducted by the University of Kansas Institute for Policy and Social Research:

Men

1.	Medicine or dentistry graduate degree	$5.25 million
2.	Business graduate degree	$2.91 million
3.	Law graduate degree	$2.9 million
4.	STEM graduate degree	$2.82 million
5.	STEM bachelor's degree	$2.66 million
6.	Business bachelor's degree	$2.26 million
7.	Health science bachelor's degree	$2.11 million
8.	Social science graduate degree	$1.98 million
9.	Liberal arts/humanities bachelor's degree	$1.88 million
10.	Social science bachelor's degree	$1.86 million
11.	Education master's degree	$1.86 million
12.	Liberal arts/humanities master's degree	$1.81 million
13.	Liberal arts/humanities master's degree	$1.53 million
14.	High school graduate	$1.49 million

Women

1.	Medicine or dentistry graduate degree	$2.12 million
2.	Business graduate degree	$1.89 million
3.	Law graduate degree	$1.77 million
4.	STEM graduate degree	$1.76 million
5.	STEM bachelor's degree	$1.74 million
6.	Business bachelor's degree	$1.5 million
7.	Health science bachelor's degree	$1.44 million
8.	Social science graduate degree	$1.39 million
9.	Liberal arts/humanities bachelor's degree	$1.38 million
10.	Social science bachelor's degree	$1.19 million
11.	Education master's degree	$1.05 million
12.	Liberal arts/humanities master's degree	$1 million
13.	Liberal arts/humanities master's degree	$0.98 million
14.	High school graduate	$0.73 million

Of course, fields of study that involve the creation of things or processes that make money will produce a greater income than study areas that may be interesting and timely but are not lucrative. That is, in general, degrees in computer engineering are worth far more than degrees in Austrian history, although one of the absolute smartest

men on earth, my old pal Aram Bakshian Jr.,
is a great expert in Austrian history and lives
comfortably.

WORK YOU LOVE

I would never dream of telling anyone what to
study or how to spend his or her working life. The
years and hours occupied by work are an immense
part of life. One should not spend them working
at a job one hates. Life is not all about how much
money you make. It is largely about enjoying one-
self and feeling pride in one's work. The matter of
enjoying the great segment of life that we spend at
work is one of life or death—we might as well be
prisoners as work in jobs we loathe.

I can vividly recall when I worked as a trial lawyer in Washington, DC, long ago. I got off the bus
in the sweltering heat and humidity and headed
into my windowless prison cell of an office, bound
to work in dim light on a hopelessly lost case—a

case that the Federal Trade Commission should never have brought—against incomparably more experienced and better paid lawyers. I felt as if I were selling my life for pennies, as if I were a blood bucket for a tribe of vampires who gorged themselves on my corpuscles while I suffered. I was not quite a slave, because I did not work in a cotton field in the brutal heat and did not get lashed if my masters were angry at me. But I was an indentured servant whose life was not his own. I was literally throwing away my one and only life while I was in those stark, fiberboard-partitioned law offices.

When I escaped that prison by becoming a teacher at American University—and then, paradise on earth, University of California, Santa Cruz—I felt free. I was a whole new person. I could do what I liked doing. I was not a lab animal on a wheel. I was a soaring bird, applauded and loved by my students, making jokes, laughing, smiling, master of my immense classroom filled with adorable students. Doing what I wanted to do transformed me from a prisoner to a king.

It is a glory of life to be able to do work that one loves.

When I started writing for money, it got even better. At that point in time, I was writing and teaching at the same time, and because I loved what I was doing, I worked tirelessly. I was creative. I could work long hours and come up with great ideas. I made more money than I ever could have by doing work I hated.

Yes, absolutely, lawyers generally make more than film teachers and movie and TV critics. True enough. But anyone who loves his work as much as I loved mine will work like a myrmidon (look it up). So I took on ever more work—work that was play compared with the horror show of legal practice. And I made more money than a starting lawyer would make by a lot.

The point is not about the legal profession. It's not about the subject of your work. It's about whether or not you enjoy it. Your humble servant will always advise working at what one loves. It's a cliché, but it's true—the money will follow, and if it doesn't, you still get the tax-free enjoyment of each day. Look at the faces of summer camp counselors and the faces of men on Wall Street and you'll get an idea of what I am talking about.

To be sure, there are men and women who love the toils of the law. They love reading the cases, the arguments and the insults, the careful craftsmanship of documents. They feel happy in a law office. I had brilliant colleagues while working as a lawyer and I enjoyed them. I am sure many lawyers feel that way about their work.

At a certain point later in my life, I became a bit of an expert on securities law and fiduciary duties of officers of corporations held by stockholders. I worked long hours reading documents regarding stock and bond offerings and annual filings with the Securities and Exchange Commission. I actually enjoyed it—the more complex the better. The difference, it seems to me, was that I was doing it voluntarily, that I was doing it in my home in Malibu overlooking the ocean and that I was—by my standards—decently paid for it. And I was respected. I was qualified in case after case as an expert witness, not as a pitiful beginning lawyer. Even the cruel practitioners on the other side in depositions had to be respectful or I would (and did) walk out. I was, as the song goes, a free man in Paris.

SAVE FIRST, THEN SPEND

The key, as it relates to the advice in this slender volume, is not to work at any specific job but to work in a job you love in such a way that you can earn enough so you can save. This saving part is absolutely life and death, and if I say it over and over, that's why.

Making sure you have enough savings is the platform for the whole rest of your life. This takes some thinking about. As the great investment genius Phil DeMuth says, "It's not about spending so you have something left over to save. It's about saving first and then allowing yourself to spend."

This is not automatic by any means. It takes discipline and what the shrinks call "reality testing."

You cannot live like a rising executive at Goldman Sachs if you are working as a librarian at your county library for the homeless. But whether you are at a library or at a Bloomberg terminal, you must arrange your life from the very get-go so that you are spending less than you earn.

This is not just important; it's vital. Only if you can adjust your life such that you save from a young age can you hope to get to the first rungs of financial nirvana.

To put it in terms that an economist would use, the idea is to convert labor into financial capital. This concept is a bit more complex than it seems and the magnitudes are incredibly vast. Long ago, I discussed this with a true superbraino at Harvard Law School, my brilliant law school classmate Duncan Kennedy. He said, with his usual smile, "It's simple. Work and save."

He's right, as he always is, but it's the magnitudes and the methods that are tricky. Once one has slain the dragon of compulsive overspending, how does one go about saving the right amount? What is the right amount?

The answer is that *no one knows*. We do know that we want to have enough saved for crises and emergencies during our working years. We know that we don't want to be on the street in a homeless encampment if our employers suddenly go belly-up. And we certainly know that we should have enough saved so that by our thirties we can live for at the very least a year without working. That's as basic as can be. That's the easy part—saving for temporary emergencies.

If you do not have enough saved so that you can live decently for a year if your boss comes into work in a grumpy mood, you are in for huge trouble. You must have that amount saved. It's not a question of "if." You must have that in a readily available, liquid-assets form.

And here, once again, is a digression.

BEFORE YOU BUY A HOME

Yes, owning a home is great. I own a lot of them, a criminally large amount of them, and I love them all. But when disaster strikes, as it did for me when I lost my job in DC at the White House because my president—Richard M. Nixon, the peacemaker—lost his job, I was in deep trouble. My friend Pat had talked me into buying a house I really could not afford. I was tapped out from the down payment—not only tapped out, but I had borrowed money from my parents and from Pat. "Liquid assets" would have been a glorious phrase for me. Instead of that tiny house in Wesley Heights, Washington, DC, I would have been happier with money in the bank. When I was called by Donald Rumsfeld and told to look for a new job or they would find me a new job, I was terrified.

I got through it by renting out my house and working like that same old myrmidon from when I moved to New York to work at the *Wall Street Journal*, writing articles, novels, anything that paid a buck. Soon, I had repaid everyone and was saving again. But those few months of constant horror at my lack of savings were indelible and wretched. It's a terrible thing to be seriously short of money. Not just short in a paranoid, unrealistic way, but genuinely short of money.

Do yourself a favor: have plenty of liquid assets before you buy a home. Liquid assets equal freedom, as my famous father said. As you get older and your expenses grow, make sure you have even more liquid assets. You can still be fired at any time. It sure looks as if all of us are going to be fired pretty soon and replaced by robots. We must have sufficient liquid assets, and I will get to the form they should take soon enough. (The short answer is short-term bonds, cash, and stocks. The longer answer is the key, though. Wait for it.)

PREPARING FOR RETIREMENT

What most of us are saving for, after we have enough liquid assets to tide us over, is retirement.

The human animal is not made to work indefinitely. We wear out. We get tired. We want to lie in bed with our spouses and our dogs. We want a change that includes leisure. Plus, our employers will want to replace our old, cranky, complaining bodies with young, energetic bodies who know how to use the latest technology and cost less per hour than we do. So the day will come when we have to leave our desks or work spaces and move out to pasture.

That's unless you own your own business. Then you can determine how long or short our work life is. That's yet another benefit of capitalism. Being your own boss is a truly immense benefit of the capitalist system.

But even if you own your own business, you will probably get tired. You will want to spend your days resting, and that requires savings. Of course, you may be able to sell your own business and live off the proceeds. But that takes us back to the whole "pre-dad" question: how do you get to a position where even if you are a salaried or hourly worker, you essentially have your own business and can sell it for enough to retire on?

We come back to our pal Duncan Kennedy: "Work and save." But how much do we save, and how do we save it?

Again, I am going to tell you what few other financial writers will tell you. I don't have the answer to part one of the question. We just know we have to save a lot, but we have no idea of how much except within broad parameters.

We know we want to have enough saved so that after retirement we can live decently—not necessarily enough to live on a yacht or in a beach house in Tahiti. We just need an amount that allows us to continue living at roughly the level we are accustomed to.

Some people believe that their spending will come down dramatically after they retire. Sometimes that happens and sometimes it doesn't. You may actually want to travel more, entertain more, and eat out more after you retire. You may want new clothes and a new computer (although those cost very little these days). But these are hopes more than a plan, and as Hillary Clinton famously said, "Hope is not a plan."

So, say if we are earning $100,000 per year now, we might expect to want to earn—by our investments, our pension, and our Social Security—roughly $100,000 the first year we retire. That's basic.

The big problems come in when we realize the following:

1. We don't have any idea whether we will actually live to retirement age. But we will assume we do, otherwise there would be little purpose in even talking about retirement.

2. We don't know how long we will live after retirement. If we assume that we will live until we are a hundred and we retire at age sixty-five, we will need a very large sum on which to retire. If we assume we will live until we are seventy-two (my age), we are going to need a lot less. There are actuarial tables that will tell you how long you can expect to live—for males and females—once you have reached a certain

age. I have included many of those at the end of this book. Read them and weep. It doesn't look good, no matter which way you look at it.

3. We don't know how much prices will rise between now and the time we retire. That is, we have no clue what the inflation rate will be from the time we start saving for retirement until the day we retire. Yes, we know the history of inflation in the post-war era, and we can say we know inflation raises prices at roughly 3 percent per year. That has been the experience since V-J Day in 1945. But bear in mind, I said *roughly*, and I meant it. There have been times when the rate of inflation has been much higher than 3 percent (say, in the 1970s) and times when it's been much lower (say, right now).

   If inflation rears its ugly head, we don't know if we will need a little more or vastly more.

Very importantly, we don't know how much inflation there will be after we retire either. If we are all set on our birthdays at age sixty-six, and suddenly inflation starts to skyrocket, we could be in trouble. Again, bear in mind, we do not know this future inflation number. It is not given to man or woman to know the future.

No one in 1959 or even 1964 would have predicted superhigh inflation in the 1970s. No one would have guessed that with the immense money creation of the Obama postcrash era we would still have very low inflation. Yet these episodes happened, and they packed a wallop. At the end of this book are tables showing how much the consumer price index has risen in every year since 1945. It's astonishing, at least to me, how much variation there has been. The rate of inflation is a variable over which we have no control, and we cannot predict it with any meaningful precision.

And it has tremendous stopping power. If prices rise by 2 percent a year and you retire at 65, they will double by the time you are 101. If prices rise by 4 percent a year, they will roughly double by the time you are 83. That can change your way of life considerably.

Factor in the giant unknown of inflation as just that: an unfathomably large monster ready to jump out of the dark forest of the future and bite you.

4. Then add some more unknowns . . . We do not know the rate of return on our investments. We can say that the rate of return has historically been 8 percent on common stocks in the postwar period, if we include reinvestment of dividends. But we have no clear idea of whether that rate will continue in the future. There have been long periods, such as 1966–72,

when there has been almost no upward movement in the major indices. But there have also been times when we have seen returns in the high teens. As I write this, we are going through a huge increase in stock prices. We don't know exactly why, and we don't know if it will continue for long. It's called the "Trump bubble," and that word *bubble* does not sound good. Trees do not grow to the sky, so it cannot continue for a terribly long time, but it certainly can continue. When it corrects, we don't know how much it will fall or how long the fall will go on.

My braino father said many times, "If something cannot go on forever, it will stop." We just don't know whether it stops with a mild sigh or with screams of pain.

5. We don't know what the rate of taxation will be. I am writing this in the winter of 2016, shortly after Mr. Donald Trump shocked many pundits when he won the

election for president. He has proposed
immense cuts in taxes for highly paid
people. Who would have even dared to
predict that Mr. Trump would be in the
Oval Office, with a GOP Congress, and
might actually be able to make those
cuts happen? Who would have predicted
it even as of Labor Day 2016? But it
happened, and we have no idea if in the
winter of 2020 we will be wondering how
Bernie Sanders won on his promise of
tripling taxes on high-income persons.
We just do not know the future.

Yet taxes are a staggeringly big factor
in Americans' lives. We have no way of
knowing what they will be in the future,
which makes planning difficult at best.

6. We don't know what personal and family
emergencies will come up that require
us to spend more money than we had
planned. A terrible crisis in a child's or
grandchild's health could have serious

effects on our spending even as we are retired or racing toward retirement. A spouse's need for long-term care can be devastating to our finances. These things not only can happen, but they do happen. Look around and see how many people you know, or their parents, who are coping with someone's senile dementia and you'll get an idea of how uncertain the future is. It can happen to you.

7. In other words, there is a helluva lot that is basically unknowable. I am sure I have missed many other factors.

How do we deal with this? Again, we hook up our lives to the mighty engine of capitalism. We don't just save by putting money into a passbook savings account. We save by attaching our future to the most powerful economic engine there has ever been: free market capitalism. We do it by plugging ourselves into the socket of corporate earnings through the stock market.

This is not going to give you perfect peace of mind. It's not going to answer all the questions you have about the future. It's just the best we can do.

MAKE YOUR MONEY WORK FOR YOU

To go back to my model citizen, genius classmate Duncan Kennedy, yes, by all means, "work and save." But work as intelligently as you can and put your money to work as intelligently as you can. There is a vast amount of data on how to make your money really put in an eight-hour day for you—or maybe a twenty-four hour day. This is not a brand-new field of study. There is a mountain of good data out there—and here are a few bits of guidance.

Take advantage of all tax subsidies, as the great Frank Knight said. There is a huge subsidy in federally favored retirement accounts. As I am writing this, there are individual retirement accounts (IRAs), which are pretty much what they sound like. You can save a certain percentage of your income and deduct it from your taxable income as you save it. Right now, the percentage you can put into an IRA is about 15 percent of your income, with a limit of about $15,000. (These numbers are approximate.) If you make these deposits when you are at your peak earnings and peak tax-rate years, the savings are substantial. Heavy emphasis: we do *not* know how Mr. Donald Trump and his Congress will change this, if at all. It would be stunning if the entire program were deleted, since retirement concerns are an immense amount of the brain space of most middle-aged (prime voting years) Americans. But then it was stunning that Mr. Trump won the election.

Of course, it's not really free money. You have to pay tax on it when you withdraw it at retirement age. If you withdraw it before retirement age, you pay a hefty penalty to "the Man." At present, that means you might have to pay a penalty of about 10 percent *plus* your income tax rate on premature withdrawals from your IRA.

If you have some kind of family emergency like a chronic illness or major injury, you can withdraw without penalty, but that gets complicated fast.

But even if you do wait until retirement age, you have to pay tax on the withdrawals as you make them. They are taxed at the ordinary income tax rate for the year in which you make the withdrawal.

The thought when IRAs were first conceived of about fifty years ago was that when workers retired, their incomes would be substantially lower than they were when the workers were, well, "working." That meant there would be a substantial saving on taxes. Plus, the funds in the IRAs would be allowed to grow and compound without tax. So that would be a substantial tax benefit as well.

We do not know what future tax rates will be even a very short distance into the future. The trend has been down, down, down. But the deficit has gone up, up, up, and some day, we might have a government that decides to do the responsible thing and raise taxes to try to reduce the deficit instead of throw tax reductions at the voters in return for votes. If we ever have a president who wants to do that, and if she really wanted to attack the national debt (now at about $20 trillion), we might be facing a hefty tax increase indeed.

For now, however, with what we do know, there is a major tax subsidy for retirement savings. Take advantage of it. That's the simple part. What you do with the money . . . well, that's a bit more complex but not overly so. We'll get to it soon.

There are also 401(k)s and their ilk. These are plans in which the preretiree pays money into an account jointly filled up with his or her employer. The money that the employee puts in is tax deferred. The money that compounds is tax deferred. However, this is a bit of a disappointment, in many cases, because the money you invest must be put into a selection of funds controlled by the employer and chosen by the employer. These may well not be the funds you would have chosen if you had free choice. Employers choose funds for 401(k)s or 401(k)-like investments based on motives that are sometimes hard to figure out. More on that later.

Then there are tax-deferred savings accounts for college and other higher-education plans. These are used by only a small fraction of the population, and they do not aim at the eight-hundred-pound gorilla in the room—retirement. So we'll just pass those by.

However, the biggest and most powerful tax tool for you is the one that has made Warren Buffett and many others terribly rich: converting short-term taxable income into long-term, *very* highly tax-advantaged capital gains income. This is the crux of my little book.

The glorious complex that leads to becoming "pre-dad"—becoming the most envied of barn-yard animals, the capitalist pig—by saving in the most intelligent way possible, by using tax advantages on a massive scale as they existed under President Obama and are likely to grow under Mr. Trump, and by hooking up to the most potent moneymaking machine in human history, the corporation, is simply this: from the earliest possible age you can do so, buy and hold common stocks in a large variety of public corporations in the United States of America and hold onto them until you retire and need the income they provide by selling them.

Here's how this miracle of tax savings works: If you buy stock in a successful corporation—and the ones that are large and have been around for a while are almost all successful—you buy a claim on the dividends that these corporations pay out year by year, quarter by quarter.

You get the pleasure of having the money jingle in your pocket, but you also have to pay tax on it. The rate on dividends has fluctuated wildly over the recent past, but let's say it's 25 percent, just as an approximation.

If you have the stock of the typical large corporation, the corporation will pay only a small fraction of the corporation's income in dividends. It reinvests the rest in machinery, or factories, or minerals, or leases, or anything it wishes to buy. In a *very* general way, this adds to the "book value" of the corporation. The "book value" is (again, very generally) the assets of the corporation minus the liabilities.

This book value grows inside the corporation like a baby inside its mother. It is not taxed as it grows . . . except in very rare instances. (There were stabs at it in World War II when the government was desperate for revenue and instituted a retained profits tax, which actually predated the war by a while and outlived it briefly. . . . I know, too much information.)

This book value can fall, as when there are economic downturns and accountants mark down the value of the assets while the size of liabilities—money the corporation owes—stays the same or grows.

But over substantial periods, book value grows. You can research how book value grows at www.gurufocus.com.

So you are accumulating a fistful of stocks over the years and decades of your work life. You don't own all, or even a meaningful share, of a large corporation. But you own a tiny percentage of the total value of a number of stocks that become an extremely meaningful part of your net worth. If you do this in the proper dimensions—which means as much as you can—you soon have an asset larger in value than your home.

This asset grows more or less trouble-free. Whenever I discuss acquiring assets with dentists or oculists who say that instead of stock they buy duplexes and fourplexes, many of them insist that rental housing is superior to stocks because you are your own CEO and don't have to pay outrageous wages to managers. They're totally right. They, the rental real estate owners, are the CEOs, treasurers, and chief operating officers themselves. That's fine for them. But they also are the plumbers, electricians, sheriffs, and hate objects of their tenants.

They don't have to worry about the day-to-day fluctuations of the stock market and about stock market panics. That's a load off of their minds. But they do have to answer calls at three in the morning from the police about shootouts at their fourplexes. They have to unclog toilets while they're on their way to their children's weddings. They have to get bat dung out of the crawl space in the attic. They have to identify bodies. They have to receive death threats when they participate in evictions.

To me, this saving of time and fear is meaningful. To me, knowing that my tenants are not going to be smoking cigars so horrible that their stench wrecks every cubic inch of the apartment is worth a lot. Not having to fear that my tenant will shoot at me when I come to politely ask for the rent—that's worth something too.

And while the property barons don't have to worry about moment-by-moment changes in their rental unit values, the values of their units can and does move up and down furiously, usually over events like recessions, crime waves, or demographic changes. Tenants can and do skip town owing months of rent. It's as if you owned a stock that pays a dividend—maybe. Most large corporations pay their dividends like clockwork. The same cannot be said of that college dropout who just signed the lease for your apartment. If you are depending on rent to service the mortgage, you can be in real trouble. Obviously, most tenants will be solid citizens. But the ones who are not can ruin your day—day after day. I know this is true. It's happened to me in one of the best neighborhoods in Aspen, Colorado.

And again, yes, you won't see day-to-day panics in rental real estate values. But real estate prices move plenty, and often in painful ways for the owners. There are such things as long-term plateaus and even downward slopes in rental property values. There are down years and even down decades for rental owners. They are rare, but they happen. Rentals can be great stuff and often are. But there are no perfect real estate models (nor perfect models of any other investment good).

LIQUID ASSETS = ACTION

Here's the huge advantage of stocks: they have perfect liquidity. Their owners can convert them to cash in less than a minute when they need money, and that liquidity is a gorgeous thing. Stocks have it; rental real estate does not. This is a big thing. When you need money in a hurry and cannot get it, you suffer. That does not happen with publicly traded stocks.

It happens a great deal of the time with real property. Liquidity is a marvelous gift; ignore it at your peril. My beloved father, the genius economist Herbert Stein, told me that one of the key lessons of life is simply this: liquid assets equal freedom. This is so true at two in the morning, when fear of financial insecurity makes its evil way into your brain.

To be sure, rental real estate is a great thing: providing tax advantages, the ability to build wealth, the capacity to absorb family members' work efforts, sometimes pride of ownership. But the aggravation and illiquidity of it frighten me. I have some rental real estate. In fact, a good chunk of my assets are in real property rentals in the form of ministore warehouses (i.e., LAACO). But these are all in the form of publicly traded REITs (real estate investment trusts) or public partnerships.

Another item: Owners of rental real estate often brag about how the value of their units goes up as their rents rise. That's completely true, but those rents are fully taxable (although with many deductions). The buildup of book value in your stocks is not taxable at all until you sell. That's a major gift.

Now hear this: all kinds of factors affect the price at which your common stocks sell: the appeal of competing securities such as bonds; the interest rate, which greatly influences the value of future earnings; macroeconomic events like waves of fear or optimism. But generally, and over very long periods, the value of your stocks is correlated to a large extent with its book value. If you don't believe me—and why should you?—believe Warren Buffett. There is a reason he includes tables of the growth of book value of his BRK (Berkshire

Hathaway) in the beginning of every annual report. He is happy when it goes up; he knows he's getting richer. The same applies to you. That means your stocks tend to go up over time as their book value more or less magically grows. Again, this is a generality, and it's rough around the edges, but it's very important.

So your investment in common stocks tends to grow, tax deferred, for as long as you own the stock. There are exceptions and long, dismal periods. Sometimes these are extremely long and extremely dismal, and I have lived through them and suffered.

But over long time spans, it's true. Book value grows and the stock price grows. Meanwhile, the investment security—usually stocks—that holds that book value is as liquid as champagne. And it won't give you a hangover.

The whole stock system in present-day America is like one huge tax-deferral system with fabulous liquidity perks—an immense IRA for all investors. You ignore it or disdain it at your peril. "Take advantage of all subsidies" (again, Frank Knight, supernova economist). The whole corporate system involves an immense tax subsidy—at least so far. (When Senator Warren is inaugurated, look out below.)

CHAPTER FIVE

THE BELLY OF THE CAPITALIST PIG

Sound investing can make you very wealthy if you're not in too big a hurry.

—Warren Buffett

Now let's summarize what we've learned. Let's play make-believe. You're a mature man or woman. You're no longer employed. Social Security is a joke. Your employer stopped offering pensions or 401(k)s long ago. Or else because you did not pay attention, you did not put enough into them and they are trivial compared with your needs. Or your investment choices were poor or just unlucky. Your parents are in heaven. Your siblings would no more consider sacrificing for your comfort and security than they would have a python as a child's pet.

You are tired. You are discouraged. And you need money—and fast. You don't need it for a large sailboat or a home on the beach in the Bahamas. You need it just to pay your rent or your car payment or your son's lawyer's fees.

What do you do? Who is there to help the old you? To help good old you?

The only you that is available to help the older you is the younger or middle-age you. You have to be the one who looks out for you in your old age or when you are ill or need money for an accident or crisis.

What will the younger you have available for the older you? Where will be the means to a decent life? Why, in the belly of the capitalist pig. In being "pre-dad" to yourself. In being a capitalist and hitching yourself and your welfare up to the gleaming, mighty chariot of the corporate stock system. In attaching your future and your family's future to the mightiest engine of prosperity there has ever been—free market capitalism—and specifically, to attach yourself to that entity through the ownership of stocks. In sum, salvation lies in becoming a capitalist.

I do not for a moment say it's the only way to amass wealth and well-being. I just say it's the best, easiest way for the ordinary investor. Real estate is fine. I love real estate. But stocks are better in terms of real return and in terms of ease of management.

But! If you are smart—and we know you are—you are thinking, "Well how the heck do I know what stocks to buy—and how do you know stocks are better than other investment vehicles? Where is your data?"

I thought you would never ask. It just so happens that my best friend on this earth, Phil DeMuth, is a gifted money manager and investor. He and I have spent immense chunks of our lives discussing how to invest. We have written many books on the subject. These, along with other useful tomes on investing, are listed at the end of this book.

We were able to verify that it is possible to build a solid moneymaking portfolio of stocks, bonds, and cash so simple that no one has any excuse at all for not doing something at least somewhat like it.

I don't want to hog the credit for these "discoveries." Others far smarter than I am have made similar findings that show how an amateur investor with little time or no education in finance can make excellent returns in the stock market over very long periods of time . . . and even over medium lengths of time.

We—along with others in the field—have found that in some ways inexperience and lack of innovation can be a major plus for investors.

I will now explain why. It has been proven beyond the shadow of a doubt that over time, investors who do not trade, who do not read and follow newsletters, who do not pay for expensive advisors, can get great returns just by "buying the market."

It is not necessary to spend hours on the computer researching stocks (although if it amuses you, go for it). All you have to do is buy and hold an "index" of all the largest stocks in the United States of America and hold onto them and add to them regularly. If possible, you should add a steadily increasing amount each month or quarter or year.

You can just go to a Merrill Lynch or a Vanguard or an Oppenheimer or a Fidelity and tell the woman at the desk that you want to open an account that holds as its primary asset an index fund (or an exchange traded fund, which is similar). The index fund will hold all five hundred stocks in the Standard & Poor's 500 Industrial Stock Index. You will own a microscopic part of all the largest companies in America. You don't ever have to trade. You don't have to check the prices hour by hour or even year by year. You just buy the index and hold onto it and add money to it.

Yes, there are fabulously smart, well-paid men and women on Wall Street and in Cambridge, Massachusetts, and Greenwich, Connecticut, who minutely study stocks. Yes, they are hardworking, well-educated people. Yes, they are trying to do their best for their investors. But the amazing truth is that these people, who manage money, who pick stocks for immense investment vehicles, are beaten in performance by the plain-old indexes about 80 percent of the time.

This apparently first came to the attention of Wall Street after World War II. A broker who could buy stocks without commission went off to war. Just for laughs, he bought one share of every stock on the New York Stock Exchange, at that time by far the largest stock market in the world. When he came back, he asked a colleague who was looking after the investment if he had any money left. To the soldier's amazement, he learned that his investment of stocks chosen totally at random, with zero research, had become an immense amount of money. It had far outperformed the funds and accounts being managed by the well-paid men in the J. Press suits.

I don't know if this story is true, and I don't care. What we do know is that extremely brilliant scholars of finance, especially a stellar genius named Burton Malkiel of Princeton, have studied the subject extensively. He and many others have found that, while there may be a few superstars who can pick stocks and get better results than you would by just buying the index, generally you will do better buying and holding the index. Just buy it, keep adding to it, and forget about it. Don't feel bad about those well-paid analysts. They'll get along somehow.

Let me be clear once again. My pal Phil DeMuth and I have worked out complex portfolios involving growth stocks, foreign stocks, small capitalization stocks, and stocks that are enjoying good momentum of growth.

We have been able to backtest these and find that they outperform the index—although not by a huge amount. To construct these portfolios has been a colossal task, with 99 percent of the work done by Dr. DeMuth. But the problem with them is that they require a great deal of work (or at least some work) to keep them finely tuned and running like a vintage Lamborghini.

For most of us, that's too much trouble. "The best is the enemy of the good," my old ma used to say. If you aim for perfection, you usually will get far less than simply very good.

With the index investment, you get very good returns over long periods, and it's so simple that you can and will stay the course. It's so simple that anyone can do it—you can and you must.

If you have time, take a peek at some of the books listed hereafter by Phil DeMuth and me (99 percent of the work done by Phil, again). And if you really want to be impressed, read Professor Burton Malkiel's masterwork, *A Random Walk Down Wall Street*. It is as close to a bible on investing as there has ever been.

Again, I intend no disrespect to stock pickers. I intend nothing but respect to money managers. I know lots of them, and they are uniformly fine fellows and women. They really want to help you.

The sad truth is that they almost never do. Don't try to outguess the market. Just buy the S&P, stay with it, and laugh all the way to the bank.

I agree; it sounds hard to believe. But it's true. Those billionaire hedge fund guys, those men and women in tailor-made clothes, will find reasons to tell you that you can and must listen to them. And maybe you should listen. But you should buy the index unless you are a sophisticated man or woman. It works; it really does.

The answer to that has been helpfully given by yet another spectacular braino named Jeremy Siegel, a brilliant shining light at Wharton, the fine business school that is part of the University of Pennsylvania. Dr. Siegel has written a book that is required reading for serious investors. I'll summarize it right now by paraphrasing the ultragod of investing, Warren E. Buffett, once again: "My preferred holding period is forever."

The data are overwhelming: over periods of time roughly commensurate to a typical working woman's life, an index of common stocks very much outperforms bonds or cash—the two alternative investments most usually thought of for people to use.

Yes, there will be terribly cruel downtimes. Yes, there will be times when stocks seem to be so high that you will think you can only get crushed if you buy in then.

But over long periods, if you keep holding on and keep buying (and always remember that a hold is as good as a buy, as the cofounder of Litton Industries, Roy L. Ash, used to tell me), you will come out far ahead of where you would be with just bonds or, worse, if you tried to rejigger your portfolio constantly to adjust to what will certainly be temporary periods when it seems insane to hold.

I am not going to reinvent the wheel here. Dr. Siegel has made his point powerfully in one best-selling edition after another. The book is called *Stocks for the Long Run*. That's what it's about, and if you read it, you will be awed.

CHAPTER SIX

CONCLUSION

It is not from the benevolence of the butcher, the brewer, or the baker that we expect our dinner, but from their regard to their own self-interest. We address ourselves not to their humanity but to their self-love, and never talk to them of our own necessities, but of their advantages.

—Adam Smith, *The Wealth of Nations*

Now, as the shrinks say when we have poured out our hearts to them for years, "We may perhaps to begin."

The key lessons of this book:

1. Free market, democratic, stock market capitalism is a phenomenal system for creating freedom and wealth for societies and nations.

2. Free market, democratic, stock market capitalism is a fabulously effective way for individuals to become well-to-do and even rich.

3. The people who tell you that capitalism is an evil, exploitive system for draining the

blood of the workers and the nonwhites are lying. There is no freer, more diverse, and more equal opportunity employer than capitalism. Capitalists have no interest at all in skin color or sex. They only want to see what you can produce. If you can produce more than you cost, you get and keep a job. If you can produce a large amount of excess over your costs, you get well paid. And if you produce very much more than you cost, you get **rich**. Skin color and ancestry have nada to do with it. Capitalism is, and must be, an equal opportunity employer. The people who tell you different are deeply incorrect as a matter of theory and fact.

4. In this life, the acquisition of money is of paramount importance. In this life, the acquisition of assets that produce income is life or death. **The absolute surest, simplest, easiest way to do that is by owning a diversified index of stocks**.

5. The preferred holding period is forever.
6. There is an immense tax subsidy built into owning stock through the nontaxation of run-ups in book value until the stock is sold and also in terms of the vastly lower taxes on income from capital gains than from labor.

    Take advantage of those subsidies.
7. The goal is not to "play the market." That way lies insanity. The goal is to become "pre-dad" and end up owning your own business—made up of many infinitesimal shares of all the biggest American businesses—and Wall Street makes it supereasy to do it.

So now you know. And as to when to start, it's simple: "Begin at once and do the best you can." Jim Bellows, a Navy fighter-hero in World War II and a genuinely great editor, put it that way, and he was right.

FINAL NOTE

THE NUMBER-ONE TAX-SAVING TIP

Let your corporate income compound
without tax inside the corporation, then
pay the capital gains rate on it when you
sell.

APPENDIX A
ACTUARIAL LIFE TABLES

An actuarial life table. Also called a mortality table, or a death chart. This information is strictly statistical. It does not take into consideration any personal health information or lifestyle information. This information has been provided by the US Census and Social Security Administration.

♂ Men				♀ Women		
Age	Expected Lifetime	Years Remaining		Age	Expected Lifetime	Years Remaining
0	75.4	75.4		0	80.4	80.4
1	75.9	74.9		1	80.9	79.9
2	76	74		2	81	79
3	76	73		3	81	78
4	76	72		4	81	77
5	76	71		5	81	76
6	76	70		6	81	75
7	76.1	69.1		7	81	74
8	76.1	68.1		8	81	73
9	76.1	67.1		9	81	72
10	76.1	66.1		10	81	71
11	76.1	65.1		11	81.1	70.1
12	76.1	64.1		12	81.1	69.1
13	76.1	63.1		13	81.1	68.1
14	76.1	62.1		14	81.1	67.1
15	76.1	61.1		15	81.1	66.1
16	76.2	60.2		16	81.1	65.1
17	76.2	59.2		17	81.1	64.1
18	76.3	58.3		18	81.2	63.2
19	76.3	57.3		19	81.2	62.2
20	76.4	56.4		20	81.2	61.2
21	76.5	55.5		21	81.2	60.2

♂ Men

Age	Expected Lifetime	Years Remaining
22	76.5	55.5
23	76.6	53.6
24	76.7	52.7
25	76.8	51.8
26	76.9	50.9
27	76.9	49.9
28	77	49
29	77.1	48.1
30	77.1	47.1
31	77.2	46.2
32	77.3	45.3
33	77.3	44.3
34	77.4	43.4
35	77.4	42.5
36	77.4	41.5
37	77.6	40.6
38	77.7	39.7
39	77.8	38.8
40	77.8	37.8
41	77.9	36.9
42	78	36
43	78.1	35.1

♀ Women

Age	Expected Lifetime	Years Remaining
22	81.3	59.3
23	81.3	58.3
24	81.3	57.3
25	81.4	56.4
26	81.4	55.4
27	81.4	54.4
28	81.4	53.4
29	81.5	52.5
30	81.5	51.5
31	81.5	50.5
32	81.6	49.6
33	81.6	48.6
34	81.6	47.6
35	81.7	46.7
36	81.7	45.7
37	81.8	44.8
38	81.8	43.8
39	81.9	42.9
40	81.9	41.9
41	82	41
42	82	40
43	82.1	39.1

♂ Men			♀ Women		
Age	Expected Lifetime	Years Remaining	Age	Expected Lifetime	Years Remaining
44	78.2	34.2	44	82.2	38.2
45	78.3	33.3	45	82.2	37.2
46	78.5	32.5	46	82.3	36.3
47	78.6	31.6	47	82.4	35.4
48	78.7	30.7	48	82.5	34.5
49	78.8	29.8	49	82.6	33.6
50	79	29	50	82.7	32.7
51	79.2	28.2	51	82.8	31.8
52	79.3	27.3	52	82.9	30.9
53	79.5	26.5	53	83	30
54	79.7	25.7	54	83.1	29.1
55	79.9	24.9	55	83.3	28.3
56	80.1	24.1	56	83.4	27.4
57	80.3	23.3	57	83.5	26.5
58	80.5	22.5	58	83.7	25.7
59	80.7	21.7	59	83.8	24.8
60	80.9	20.9	60	84	24
61	81.2	20.2	61	84.1	23.1
62	81.4	19.4	62	84.3	22.3
63	81.7	18.7	63	84.5	21.5
64	81.9	17.9	64	84.7	20.7
65	82.2	17.2	65	84.9	19.9

♂ Men			♀ Women		
Age	Expected Lifetime	Years Remaining	Age	Expected Lifetime	Years Remaining
66	82.5	16.5	66	85.1	19.1
67	82.8	15.8	67	85.3	18.3
68	83.1	15.1	68	85.6	17.6
69	83.4	14.4	69	85.8	16.8
70	83.7	13.7	70	86.1	16.1
71	84.1	13.1	71	86.3	15.3
72	84.4	12.4	72	86.6	14.6
73	84.8	11.8	73	86.9	13.9
74	85.2	11.2	74	87.2	13.2
75	85.6	10.6	75	87.6	12.6
76	86	10	76	87.9	11.9
77	86.5	9.5	77	88.3	11.3
78	86.9	8.9	78	88.6	10.6
79	87.4	8.4	79	89	10
80	87.9	7.9	80	89.4	9.4
81	88.4	7.4	81	89.9	8.9
82	88.9	6.9	82	90.3	8.3
83	89.5	6.5	83	90.8	7.8
84	90.1	6.1	84	91.3	7.3
85	90.1	5.7	85	91.8	6.8
86	91.3	5.3	86	92.3	6.3
87	91.9	4.9	87	92.9	5.9

♂ Men			♀ Women		
Age	Expected Lifetime	Years Remaining	Age	Expected Lifetime	Years Remaining
88	92.6	4.6	88	93.5	5.5
89	93.2	4.2	89	94.1	5.1
90	93.9	3.9	90	94.7	4.7
91	94.6	3.6	91	95.4	4.4
92	95.4	3.4	92	96	4
93	96.2	3.2	93	96.8	3.8
94	96.9	2.9	94	97.5	3.5
95	97.8	2.8	95	98.3	3.3
96	98.6	2.6	96	99.1	3.1
97	99.4	2.4	97	99.9	2.9
98	100.3	2.3	98	100.7	2.7
99	101.2	2.2	99	101.5	2.5
100	102.1	2.1	100	102.4	2.4

APPENDIX B
CONSUMER PRICE INDEX

By looking at the change in the Consumer Price Index (CPI) we can see that an item that cost an average of 18 cents in 1945 would cost us about $1.84 in 2003, $2.07 in 2007, $2.33 in 2013 and $2.40 in 2016. This data is supplied by the Bureau of Labor Statistics.

Year	CPI ($)	Year	CPI ($)
1945	.18	1969	.37
1946	.19	1970	.39
1947	.22	1971	.40
1948	.24	1972	.42
1949	.24	1973	.44
1950	.24	1974	.50
1951	.26	1975	.54
1952	.27	1976	.57
1953	.27	1977	.60
1954	.27	1978	.65
1955	.27	1979	.73
1956	.27	1980	.82
1957	.28	1981	.91
1958	.29	1982	.96
1959	.29	1983	1.00
1960	.30	1984	1.04
1961	.30	1985	1.08
1962	.30	1986	1.10
1963	.30	1987	1.14
1964	.31	1988	1.18
1965	.32	1989	1.24
1966	.32	1990	1.31
1967	.33	1991	1.36
1968	.35	1992	1.40

Year	CPI ($)	Year	CPI ($)
1993	1.44	2006	2.02
1994	1.48	2007	2.07
1995	1.52	2008	2.15
1996	1.57	2009	2.14
1997	1.60	2010	2.18
1998	1.63	2011	2.25
1999	1.67	2012	2.30
2000	1.72	2013	2.33
2001	1.77	2014	2.37
2002	1.80	2015	2.37
2003	1.84	2016	2.40
2004	1.89	2017	2.44
2005	1.95		

GLOSSARY

401(k): An employer-sponsored retirement savings plan allowing employees to save and invest a portion of their paychecks before taxes are taken out. Taxes aren't paid until the money is withdrawn from the account.

Aram Bakshian Jr.: Noted aide to presidents Nixon, Ford, and Reagan. His writings on politics, history, gastronomy, and the arts are widely published.

Barron's: In print and digital editions, this financial weekly has been a must-read for investors and Wall Street since 1921.

Berkshire Hathaway: With Warren Buffett as CEO and Charlie Munger as vice-chairman, this is an American multinational conglomerate holding company headquartered in Omaha, Nebraska. Holdings include GEICO, BNSF Railway, Lubrizol, Dairy Queen, Fruit of the Loom, Helzberg Diamonds, FlightSafety International, Pampered Chef, and NetJets, as well as 43.63 percent of the Kraft Heinz Company, an undisclosed percentage of Mars, Incorporated, and significant minority holdings in American Express, the Coca-Cola Company, Wells Fargo, IBM, Restaurant Brands International, and Apple. Berkshire Hathaway averaged an annual growth in book value of 19.7 percent for the last half-century (compared to 9.8 percent from the S&P 500 for the same period) while employing large amounts of capital and incurring minimal debt.

book value: The total amount a company would be worth if it liquidated its assets and paid back all its liabilities.

Warren Buffett: CEO of Berkshire Hathaway and known as the "Oracle of Omaha," Buffett is an investment guru and one of the richest and most respected businessmen in the world. His annual letters to shareholders are must-read sources of investing wisdom each year for individual investors and Wall Street alike.

bureaucrat: A nonelected government official, often perceived as being concerned with procedural correctness at the expense of people's needs.

capital: Financial assets, or the value of financial assets.

capital gains: The profit from the sale of property or of an investment.

capitalism: An economic and political system in which private owners control trade and industry for profit.

Philip DeMuth: A psychologist and registered investment advisor who holds a master's degree and a PhD from the University of California at Santa Barbara. DeMuth has written for the *Wall Street Journal*, *Barron's*, the *Louis Rukeyser Newsletter*, and Forbes.com, as well as *Human Behavior* and *Psychology Today*. He is the author of numerous books, including several coauthored with Ben Stein.

distribution: The movement of goods and services through a source to the final consumer.

economic freedom: The freedom to produce, trade, and consume any goods and services acquired without the use of force, fraud, or theft.

economics: The social science concerned with the production, consumption, and transfer of wealth.

feudal system: Economic and political system in which a peasant or worker known as a vassal received a piece of land in return for serving a lord or king. Vassals were expected to perform various duties in exchange for their own fiefs, or areas of land.

free market: An economic system in which prices are determined by unrestricted competition among privately owned businesses.

Milton Friedman: Nobel Prize–winning economist (1976) and advisor to Republican U.S. president Ronald Reagan and Conservative British prime minister Margaret Thatcher. His political philosophy extolled the virtues of a free market economic system with minimal intervention. He is the author of numerous influential books, monographs, and articles including the seminal work *Capitalism and Freedom*.

index fund: A type of mutual fund with a portfolio that matches components of market indexes such as the Standard & Poor's 500 Index

(S&P 500). These funds generally provide broad market exposure, low operating expenses, and low portfolio turnover.

inflation: A general increase in prices and fall in the purchasing value of money. You get less for your money.

IRA: An individual retirement account (IRA) allows individuals to direct pretax income toward investments that can grow tax deferred; capital gains or income tax is paid only when funds are withdrawn.

Duncan Kennedy: A founding member of the Critical Legal Studies movement, he is the Carter Professor of General Jurisprudence at Harvard Law School.

Frank Knight: Along with Milton Friedman (among others), one of the founders of the "Chicago school of economics" with a belief that free markets and limited governmental intervention are best at allocating resources in society.

limited liability corporation (LLC): A corporation (company) whose members cannot be held personally liable for the company's debts or liabilities.

means of production: The facilities and resources for producing goods.

money: The assets, property, and resources owned by someone or something; wealth.

pension: A regular payment made during a person's retirement from an investment fund to which the employer has contributed during that person's working life.

price action: The movement of a security's (stock's) price.

real estate investment trust (REIT): A company that owns or finances income-producing real estate; modeled after mutual funds.

regulation: The imposition of rules by government, backed by the use of penalties that are intended specifically to modify the economic behavior of individuals and firms in the private sector.

scarcity of goods: A good or resource with limited availability that is in high demand.

stocks and shares: A stock is a general term used to describe the ownership certificates of any company. A share, on the other hand, refers to the stock certificate of a particular company. Holding a particular company's share makes you a shareholder.

subsidies: Money granted by the government or a public body to assist an industry or business so that the price of a commodity or service may remain low or competitive.

tax-deferred income: Investments on which applicable taxes (typically income taxes and capital gains taxes) are paid at a future date instead of in the period in which they are incurred.

trade protectionism: A policy of restraining trade between countries through methods such as tariffs on imported goods, restrictive quotas, and a variety of other government regulations.

value investing: An investing strategy where stocks selected are ones that investors feel have been undervalued by the market.

FURTHER READING

John C. Bogle. *Little Book of Commonsense Investing: The Only Way to Guarantee Your Fair Share of Stock Market Returns* (2007).

Mary Buffett and David Clark. *The Tao of Warren Buffett: Warren Buffett's Words of Wisdom: Quotations and Interpretations to Help Guide You to Billionaire Wealth and Enlightened Business Management* (2006).

Warren Buffett. *Berkshire Hathaway Shareholder Letters, 1965–2014* (2016); also available on

the Berkshire Hathaway website: http://www
.berkshirehathaway.com/letters/letters.html.

Warren Buffett and Lawrence A. Cunningham.
*The Essays of Warren Buffett: Lessons for Corpo-
rate America* (2015 edition).

Phil DeMuth. *The Affluent Investor: Financial
Advice to Grow and Protect Your Wealth* (2013)

Milton Friedman. *Capitalism and Freedom* (1962),
reissued 2002.

Benjamin Graham. *The Intelligent Investor: The
Definitive Book on Value Investing. A Book of
Practical Counsel* (1949), reissued in 2006.

Benjamin Graham and David L. Dodd. *Security
Analysis*, 6th ed. (originally published in 1934),
reissued in 2008 with a foreword by Warren
Buffett and commentary by leading investing
experts.

Edwin Lefèvre. *Reminiscences of a Stock Operator* (1923), reissued in 2006.

Burton G. Malkiel. *A Random Walk Down Wall Street: The Time-Tested Strategy for Successful Investing* (2016 edition).

Jeremy J. Siegel. *Stocks for the Long Run: The Definitive Guide to Financial Market Returns & Long-Term Investment Strategies* (2014 edition).

Ben Stein and Phil DeMuth. *The Little Book of Alternative Investments: Reaping Rewards by Daring to be Different* (2011).

Ben Stein and Phil DeMuth. *The Little Book of Bulletproof Investing: Do's and Don'ts to Protect Your Financial Life* (2010).

INDEX

Page numbers followed by *t* refer to tables.

ABOUT THE AUTHOR

Ben Stein studied economics and finance at Columbia university from which he graduated in 1966. He is a graduate of Yale Law School, where he also studied investing and finance. He has written extensively about investments for *Barrons*, *The New York Times*, Yahoo! Finance, and almost every other financial publication. He taught economics at Pepperdine University. He is a frequent commentator on CBS Sunday Morning and CNN and has been a regular panelist on Fox News' "Cavuto on Business" for more than ten years. Along with his friend and colleague Phil DeMuth he has written many best sellers about investing. He was the host of almost nine hundred episodes of "Win Ben Stein's Money", a show that won 7 Emmys. He is an extremely active speaker about investing and economics and has been a noted actor in movies and TV for decades.

MY NOTES

MY NOTES

MY NOTES

The Franklin Prosperity Report

Great Giveaways and Awesome Bargain Adventures
For People Over 50

Get more than 40 incredible money-saving tips that every senior should know about!

In this new **FREE** report, we reveal how to find out if you or your family is eligible for a share of the trillions of dollars in grants, services, and other goodies that Uncle Sam gives out every year.

This report is a must read for anyone looking to have more money during their retirement.

Inside this report you'll discover:

- That only 12% of the money in government "free-money" programs goes to the poor! In fact, a larger percentage of "wealthy" people than poor people are eligible for these funds . . .

- Up to three-fourths of government money programs have no income requirements. There may be money available to you no matter how much you currently make!

- Get free healthcare if you have no insurance coverage . . .

- How to sign up for free or reduced-cost prescription drugs . . .

- We even reveal 7 mistakes you must avoid making if you are low on money . . .

- Plus much more!

Get your FREE report today:

Newsmax.com/FreeTips

How an Ordinary Man Turned $8,000 Into $7 Million

GET HIS SECRETS TO WEALTH TODAY

The Dividend Machine, written by Bill Spetrino, has been hailed by Mark Hulbert of the *Hulbert Financial Digest* as the #1 low-risk newsletter in the industry, based on performance.

One look at the portfolio tells you why the newsletter deserves such acclaim. It is filled with companies from all across the globe that hold a dominant position in their industries. And these companies use that dominant position to generate piles and piles of cash, which they return to shareholders in the form of dividends.

But not just any dividend payer will qualify for inclusion in **The Dividend Machine** portfolio. In order to be added to the portfolio, it must meet a very stringent set of criteria that Bill has set forth. And it must have one final factor above all: it must be priced right.

The Dividend Machine is a culmination of more than 20 years of Bill's personal experience investing in high-quality dividend stocks. In fact, it is the exact same investing philosophy that allowed Bill to walk away from his 9-to-5 job at the age of 42 and live comfortably on the income from his investments alone.

As a member of **The Dividend Machine**, you will be partners with Bill. For only $97.95 per year, you will be able to study his analysis, learn from his insight, and gain knowledge from his vast investment experience. In short, you will have one of the world's leading experts in dividend investing working with you side-by-side every month. And each month Bill will recommend a new opportunity to consider adding to your personal Dividend Machine portfolio.

To Learn More About Partnering With Bill, Go To:
Newsmax.com/TDMCode